102 Haunted House Jokes

Ski Michaels

Library of Congress Cataloging-in-Publication Data

———
102 haunted house jokes / by Ski Michaels.
    p.   cm.
    Summary: A collection of jokes about ghosts, monsters, and
vampires.
    ISBN 0-8167-2578-0 (pbk.)
    1. Wit and humor, Juvenile.   2. Haunted houses—Juvenile humor.
[1. Jokes.   2. Ghosts—Wit and humor.   3. Wit and humor.]
I. Title.   II. Title: One hundred two haunted house jokes.
PN6163.P44   1992
818'.5402—dc20   91-21891

This edition published in 1999.

Printed in the United States of America.

10 9 8 7 6

Why don't ghosts have money problems?

They don't have to worry about the cost of living.

What do men ghosts use in the morning?

After-grave lotion.

Why was the aging monster upset?

She was starting to lose her ghoulish figure.

What do ghosts wish on at night?

Mon*stars.*

Where's the best place to build a haunted house?

On a dead-end street.

What's scary and checks houses for problems?

The building in-specter.

What did one cool ghost say to the other?

Get a life, dude!

Why did the baseball player bring a ghost to the game?

His coach told him to show some spirit.

What's scary and rescues ships?

The Ghost Guard.

Why did the broken robot become a ghost?

Because he couldn't rust in peace.

What did the referee say before the ghost boxing match?

May the best frighter win!

How do English ghosts drink tea?

With cups and sorcerers.

Who is a ghost's best friend?

His haunting dog.

What do you call a first-grade monster?

An elementary-ghoul student.

What do skeletons do before a test?

They bone up on their studies.

What do you find on the windows of a haunted house?

Shudders!

What kind of mail do ghosts like to get?

Chain letters.

What's ghostly and hops?

A boo-frog!

What kind of bugs do you find in a graveyard?

Zom-bees.

Why did the ghost go to court?

He wanted the judge to give him a life sentence.

Where do ghosts go to become pilots?

Fright school.

What room in a haunted house goes flap! flap! flap?

The bat-room.

Why did the ghost go to Hollywood?

He wanted to take a scream test.

Why couldn't the ghost keep a secret?

He was dying to tell someone.

What do ghosts rattle in winter?

Snow chains.

What does a construction ghost operate?

A boo-dozer!

What bird loves to live in a haunted house?

A screech owl.

What's spooky and goes on safaris?

A big-game haunter.

Why was the little ghost crying?

He fell down and got a boo-boo!

Why did the little ghosts have to stay after school?

They were caught frighting at recess.

What lives in a haunted house and loves the World Series?

A baseball bat.

What kind of piano did the monster play?

A Franken-Steinway.

What do you find in the freezer of a haunted house?

Ice scream.

Is it hard to clean a haunted house?

No. Dirt and grime just vanish.

Why didn't the ghoul buy a lottery ticket?

He didn't have a ghost of a chance of winning.

What is a ghost's favorite dessert?

Boo-berry pie.

What is Indiana Spook's favorite weapon?

A boo-whip!

What game do little ghosts like to play?

Hide and shriek!

Which member of the ghost hockey team wears a mask?

The ghoulie.

What do you use to catch a ghost bug?

A boo-bee trap.

Who is the loudest instructor in ghost school?

The screech teacher.

Why is a ghost like a cold breeze?

They both make people shiver.

How does a ghost address a letter?

Tomb it may concern.

What do you call the place where a monster is buried?

A fiendish plot.

What kind of ghost haunts cotton fields?

The boo-weevil!

Who's scary and cleans houses?

The Ghost Dusters.

Why should skeletons never wear shorts?

They have bony knees.

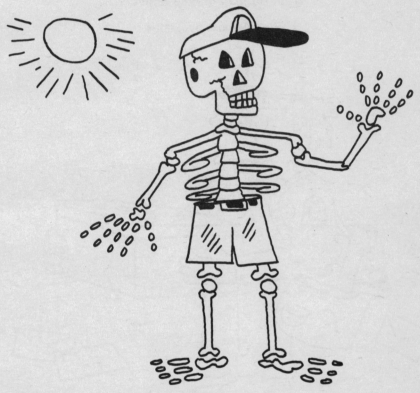

Why did the spirit dial the long-distance operator?

He wanted to make a ghost-to-ghost phone call.

What do mail ghouls deliver?

Parcel-ghost packages.

What does Dracula the Dentist use to pull teeth?

Vam-plyers.

What goes bounce! bounce! boo! boo! bounce! bounce! boo! boo?

A po-ghost stick.

What has wheels and shrieks?

A roller-ghoster.

How did the ghost get so stupid?

He was scared out of his wits.

What did the ghost say to his ghoul-friend?

Gee, you look boo-tiful!

Where do ghosts like to live?

In a frightful state.

Why do bats go to haunted houses?

Just to hang around.

What's the favorite lawn game of ghosts?

Bat-minton.

What did the cool ghoul say when he saw a grave?

Yo! Dig that!

Why was the ghost psychologist upset?

His patients had grave problems.

What floats in the air and scares airline passengers?

A hot-air boo-lloon.

Why did the ghost join the army?

He wanted to fright for his country.

What is a ghost's favorite painting?

The Moaning Lisa.

What kind of ghost goes *va-room!* when it flies?

A jet frighter.

What kind of birthday decorations do ghosts like?

Party screamers.

Why can't ghosts deceive people?

It's easy to see right through them.

Why are ghost celebrations so dull?

No one can be the life of the party.

Why should you never take ghosts to a football game?

They boo every play.

What does a ghost keep in his stable?

Nightmares!

What do ghosts wear on their feet when it rains?

*Ghoul*ashes.

Where do ghosts put up notices?

On a boo-lletin board!

What happens when ghost cowboys ride a lot of horses?

They get boo-legged.

When do ghosts go out to play?

Whenever the spirit moves them.

How can you tell if a ghost has a cold?

He keeps a coffin (coughin').

What do you get if you cross rain clouds with ghosts?

Thunder and frightening.

Why did the baseball umpire call Dracula out?

He batted out of turn.

How do you stop baby ghosts from crying?

Change their sheets.

Why did the ghost go to the marsh?

He wanted to haunt ducks.

What did the spirit say to the ghost who fainted?

Don't just lie there, shriek to me!

What's the hardest thing to sell to a ghost?

Life insurance.

What did Mad Doctor Cheese invent?

A Frankenstein munster.

What do ghosts do in the summer?

They moan their lawns.

Why did the skeleton order a pitcher of soda?

His throat was bone dry.

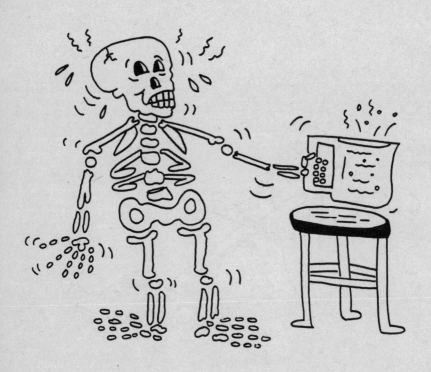

Where do you find a ghost fish?

In the Dead Sea.

What does a ghost soldier use to shoot with?

A Boo-zooka.

Who invented the ghost airplane?

Wilbur and Orville Fright.

Where are ghost motion pictures made?

In *Howl*ywood.

What Civil War general was a monster?

*Ghoul*ysses S. Grant.

What did the skeleton say to the comedian?

Please don't break me up.

Why did the ghost go to the employment office?

He was job haunting.

Why did the bat business go bankrupt?

It was a fly-by-night operation.

How do ghosts score extra points in football games?

They kick the ball over the ghoul posts.

What do you call a ghost telephone?

A dead ringer.

What's wet and spooky?

The Eerie Canal.

Which ghost works as a security guard?

The fright watchman.

Why didn't the ghost like the novel about the cemetery?

It had too many plots in it.

What do ghosts put on their salads?

Boo-cheese dressing.

Why did the skeleton go to a psychologist?

He thought he was going out of his skull.

Why did the ghost go to the beach?

He wanted to get buried in the sand.

What ghost patriot flew a kite in a storm?

Boo-jamin Franklin.

What do you call a small haunted house where ghosts live?

A boo-galow.

Do ghosts take showers?

No. They take boo-ble baths.

Why didn't the ghost go out after work?

He was dead tired.